Fulfilling Your Destiny

I0121968

"This poor man cried, and the LORD heard him, and saved him out of all his troubles." Psalms 34:6

Clifton E. Battle Sr.

UWriteit Publishing Company
Goldsboro, NC USA
www.uwriteitpublishingcompany.com

Fulfilling Your Destiny by Clifton Battle
Copyright © 2012 by Clifton Battle

ISBN: ISBN-13: **978-0615740188** (**UWriteIt Publishing Company**)
ISBN-10: **0615740189**

First Printing December – 2012

Unless otherwise indicated, Scripture quotations in this book are from the King James Version of the Bible.

This publication is designed to provide information in regard to the subject matter covered. It is published with the understanding that the authors are not engaged in rendering legal counsel or other professional services. If legal advice or other professional advice is required, the services of a professional person should be sought.

Printed in the U.S.A.

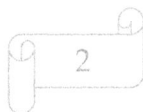

Dedication

This book is dedicated to my wife Brenda, who has given me years of love and dedication, prayer and support. Also, I dedicate this book to my mother Edna and Grandmother Lucy Swift for their prayers and support. To my lovely daughter Comeshia (meats) Battle, daddy loves you and misses you. See you one day in Heaven.

To my son Clementa (Tava-lo) Battle, I hope and pray I am that example that will change your life forever. If God did it for "pops" he can do it for you son.

Also, I like to dedicate this book to these great god fearing men, their wives and church families for coming into my life. Apostle Johnnie Washington, the founder of Tabernacle of Prayer for All People Inc. Apostle Lawrence Bogier and Eldress Coretha Bogier, The Original Tabernacle of Prayer for All People Inc. Pastor Danny and Beth Kirby of New Covenant Fellowship and the Jacob's House. Pastor Joseph and (momma) Reita Watson of The Church of God for All People. Also, Prophetess Paula Artis for the wisdom she passed down to my brother in law and he passed it down to me, thank you Prophetess Paula. I would like to give special thanks to, Melissa Hardy, Okenna Bell and Tracy Powell. I thank my niece and soon to be Professor, Jeanette W. Morris. I also thank you for your smile that has always been a great encouragement to me.

Table of Contents

1. **Brief Background**

- Family — Normal Childhood — 2nd of 13 Children

- High School Graduation

- Visit to Washington D.C.
  a. Life of Drugs, drinking, Crime, etc…
  b. Charged and Jailed

- 1973 Returned to Goldsboro
  a. Life of Drugs, Drinking, and Crime continues.
  b. Drugs Overdose
  c. Crime continues to support drug habit (Robbery, etc…)

- 1977 Salvation — Received Christ into my life.

- Marriage and Family

- 1988-A Life of Struggles and Backsliding

2. **Life Change — August 2, 1992**
  a. James Street

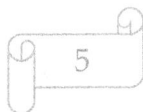

1

Background History

"This poor man cried, and the LORD heard him, and saved him out of all his troubles." Psalms 34:6

"God is good, He knows more about me than I know about myself; sin is the cause of it all."

I grew up in the small city of Goldsboro, NC. I was born second among a family of 13 children; this is where life began for me.

Living A Normal Childhood

Living a normal childhood and enjoying life as I knew it, when I was about 8 years old I played all types of sports, except golf and tennis. I played sports that made you eat a lot but food was very scares in those days. I was pretty good in everything I did and really enjoyed my life in sports.

There were two men that played a major part in my life as a youngster; one was a preacher name Mr. Matthew Snead. Mr. Snead talked me a lot of things as a kid, I remember when I was about 6 years old he had all the kids in the neighborhood and the project to come over his house for bible study and prayer. During those times I didn't understand it but that was one of his ways to help keep us out of trouble.

Mr. Snead also set us up a park with lights on Crawford Street and he set up a boxing ring. He taught us how to box, play basketball and horseshoe, he was a great mentor. He would feed the whole project with wash pots full of vegetables soup; he was the first one to plant a positive seed in my life.

The next gentlemen was Mr. T.C. Coley, words can't explain what he meant to me. Mr. Coley was a real father figure, a friend, mentor, buddy and an individual that told you, you can make something of yourself and do better in life. I remember many days of riding on the back of his truck sitting in a wooden chair going to Mina Well Park. We would travel to W.A. Foster, a popular community center in Goldsboro at that time. We traveled many miles to tournaments on that truck, Kinston, New Bern, Wilson, Tarboro etc… these were the good old days. At the end of the season we would have a picnic in the park and would receive the trophy for M.V.P. I was pretty good and the team I played on was the Celtics. I played in the midget league and we won the championship back to back at the end of the year.

T.C. would pick 10 of the best players to travel for the tournament and I was on the team for both years, there were about 50 people playing in the league. When I got to the junior league I didn't play much because the coach had favoritism and played his brother over me, we didn't go very far that year. I knew I could play and that I was supposed to be one of the starting players but I wasn't and it was there lost.

I had a cousin name (Tyrone) and he was good in every sport, you name it he could do it. He could dive (Grey Louganis) has nothing on him, (Mark Spitz) could not touch him, he use to put on diving shows, it was incredible. He could swim like a fish you had to see him to believe it. Even in basketball, he was good, all state and practically every college wanted him. He could have gone anywhere he wanted. The great (John Wooden) from UCLA (John Bibby), you think David Thompson and Michael Jordan were great, they couldn't hold water with this guy. He had a chance to play with the Washington Bullets but he couldn't handle the rigorous practices and exercise programs. He walked off the court because his life had become entangled with drugs. He allowed drugs to take over his life (you see the chains have been broken in his life). Drugs are a monster and it will eat up your life over time. He could have been a great quarterback, pitcher or anything he wanted to become but drugs was the monkey on his back.

Back in the day there was a lot to do and I enjoyed life to the fullest, sports were my passion during my youth and teenage years. When it was baseball season I played baseball and I played different positions because I was good in baseball and they called me the great (Robert Clementa) from Puerto Rico. I led the league in batting, T.C. would pick the 15 best players to travel and we won many games.

Also, I loved to swim back in the days and I was on the swimming team and my favorite stroke was the breaststroke. They would have me to swim 3 legs on the relay team. We would often jump the fence at night and go swimming at the pool and we never got caught. Life was fun back then and my junior year I played basketball but I was not good enough to make the high school team so I just played at W.A. Foster. We won the championship two years in a row, I was on a team called The Mighty Hawk, my game became very good and they would call me (Gus Williams). When the big boys got the rebound I was on the other end for the fast break. We had football players on the team and boy were they rough, no one wanted to come down the lane because if they did they knew they would get a hard foul and I mean hard. If they did come they thought about it the next time they came down the lane.

I was picked for all tournaments because I led the league in scoring that year. I thank God that I can remember it just as if it was yesterday. My mother had about 8 children at this time, seven boys and one girl. We had hard times financially growing up, I can remember coming home from school one day and when I got home all the furniture was on the street corner, I said my God what is going on. I remember that my mother had a real bad drinking problem and many times she would fall down on the streets she was so drunk. Many nights we went to bed hungry because we had no food in the house. We had our water and lights cut off so many times that when we had to use the bathroom we had to use this B1 can. Many times when we took a bath we had to use the same water, we often had to get water from our neighbor's house.

We had to go stay at our aunt and uncle's house but things weren't much better there because my mother's sister was an alcoholic also. We had to sleep on one bed, there were about 10 boys sleeping on one bed. We had to smell feet and everything, one cousin wet the bed very bad every night and we let him sleep in that same spot every night.

Let me tell you a little about my father, I loved him; he was my father (Robert Lee Swift). Back in the early 55 and 60's he had a gang called the Red Shirt Gang and boy were they mean. I can remember one day on Crawford Street a man and my father were having a shoot out machine gun style, trying to kill each other. They were hiding behind houses and it was a site to see my father in this gun fight. He could have died that day or killed that man (Townsend), it wasn't God's timing yet. My father and his gang went to Mt. Olive, put a chain on his SS Chevy and busted one of his friends out of jail. They didn't make jails back then like they do today.

I believe in my heart that if they could have made it in the city west, cast side, Harlem they were tough. The Jones family and the Swift family were in-laws one way or another. My uncle told me that we were not in the gang, but he bought a red shirt just to keep us off of him. My mother and my aunt told me some other things about my father; no one would cross Robert Lee Swift. When I tell people who my father is they ask me am I as mean as he was. They say your father was a real gangster, no one would touch him. If you were born in the 40's most people would know who he was. His brother had to leave Goldsboro early in life because he hung a white man and he couldn't go back to NC. This is not a fiction story, every word I'm telling you is true and I hope that by the time you finish reading this book you can get the real meaning of what I'm saying. I want you to know that God can do anything but fail.

The Jones family ruled Herman and Crawford St.; my father was part of that. Anyone could not just come down the street; I was an eye witness to this. I remember an incident where I saw this old lady (Jones) took the police gun and they kicked him off the force. I remember also just like it was yesterday how this man came down Crawford Street he didn't know the reputation of this street, so as young boys trying to make a name for ourselves we took him to a place called the Jungle and we put a beating on him. He will never forget that beating I guarantee you he remembers that beating today. In making a reputation for ourselves we were going to different areas being bad, projects, Phelps alley, Wilmington Ave., Herman St etc...

When we moved to Herman St. my mother got married to a man that was willing to marry her and take on her 8 kids (Jesus) he must be special or something. My mother finally stopped drinking and became a devoted wife and mother and there were added to our family 4 more girls and one boy. My mother gave her all to this man and they bought a brand new house on Herman St. He was in the army and life was good for a while and then he started cheating but my mother kept her faith in God through it all. God will not put more on you than you can bear but will make a way of escape so that you can make it through.

My father in law was also a pothead, one day he went into the barn and found a lot of marijuana that one of my brothers had hid. You think he gave it back; he smoked it and sold it around the tavern he hung at. I told him that I would not take that lying down, my father in law wanted to take me on and if it wasn't for my mother I would have taken this guy out. You don't let anyone walk over your mother like that. He left my mother with the mortgage and she couldn't pay for it so we had to let it go, but she still held on to her faith in God. My mother was a member of The Tabernacle of Prayer for All People where the Overseer was Apostle Johnnie Washington and the Pastor Lawrence Bogier. This church believed that prayer was the answer for every situation and they told my mother that she would be victorious in this situation.

High School Graduation 1969

I went to Dillard High School and I was a part of the last class to graduate from Dillard. I love the Dillard High Class Mates but little did I know that at the age of 19 my life would take a terrible turn for the worst. After graduating from high school this young country boy decided to go to the **Bright Lights.**

Visit to Washington D.C.

After I graduated from high school I took a wrong

turn in life and that was the beginning of my troubles. I went to Washington D.C. to fulfill the desires of my heart and I stayed with my aunt and uncle while I was there. Finally, I am in the big city and ready to go forth to see what city living is all about. I am ready to explore and take advantage of the opportunities that were before me.

A Life of Drugs, Drinking and Crime

I begin working as a porter at the Madison Hotel and during this time I was doing well for myself. However, I made a decision that led me on a deadly course and this would be the first of many wrong decisions. During the course of my stay with my aunt and uncle I decided to leave that beautiful home and neighborhood for my own apartment. The area that I moved in was consumed with drugs and prostitution. This is where I met two angels but they were not from heaven and neither would they lead me there. This beautiful young lady (angel) introduced me to a dust (angel) that took my life to a downward spiral and a roller coaster ride that continued for a while. This drug (angel dust) had me hallucinating to a point that I thought I was going crazy. Then this young lady (angel) took me further and deeper into darkness by introducing me to heroin and I begin snorting heroin up my nose and that lasted for a while.

This downward spiral of my life caused by drugs only got worse and I begin to use needles and that was hell on earth. After I begin to use these drugs I was fired from my job for stealing alcohol. I was using about 20 capsules of drugs a day at a cost of $1.50 per capsule. However, this soon escalated and the habit increase while my money was decreasing. I had to get the money to keep supporting my habit so I made another wrong decision and begin to engage in breaking and entering and you can imagine where this road led me.

Charged and Jailed

My life at this point was getting ready to go from bad to worse. One morning I was coming out of a drug house with 3 packs of heroin on me and I was arrested, I could not believe it, my heart fainted in me, I was arrested for drug possession. I am sitting in jail in a strange city without anyone to stand my bond and no hope of getting out. Little did I know that I was about to witness things that would shake my very being. While been contained in the holding cells I witness men raping men and men killing men over men that they believed were their property.

Finally, they came to get me and took me from the holding area to the D.C. jail and I stayed locked up for ten long weeks before my trial date came. The system even tried to take me before a disciplinary board for sodomy. I said no way I don't do that, the night before the guy sleeping next to me was raped (Jesus). But God intervened and nothing else was ever said to me about that from the board.

Do you remember earlier when I said that I took up boxing, well I had to put it to use when I went out on the yard. I was confronted by this big guy, I don't know if he was trying me or what but I let him know that he wasn't going to do anything to me. We squared off and I gave him a few body shots and after that he went about his business. The (Swift) in me came out because it had to, I went in a man and I was coming out a man and nothing in between. After been locked up for ten weeks I was placed on probation and remained in the city until my probation was over.

1973 — Returned to Goldsboro

After having my fill of drugs and the incarcerated life I decided that it was time to go back home where the living was easy, simple and away from the drug scene. To my surprise I found out that this little simple city of Goldsboro had also become infested with drugs as well. I soon came to the reality that there was nowhere to hide, so instead of going cold turkey (kicking the habit abruptly) I begin shooting up more drugs here than I did in Washington D.C... I was selling it also but I was shooting up more than I was selling. My habit got so bad that the dealer fired me himself. At this point I was doing up to $200 a day or more and do you think I stopped there? No it got worse!

Life of Drugs, Drinking and Crime Continues

The craving for drugs got even worse and I begin to carry a sawed-off shot gun and holding up drug dealers or anyone that could meet my need. I would do what I had to do and go where I had to go.

- I begin to rob stores.
- Robbing the guys in base housing.
- Taking money bag from the grocery store.
- Stealing pay roll checks.
- Breaking in Golf Courses.
- Shoplifting Murphy games.
- Snatching pocket books.
- Stealing clothes and running out of the store, no cheap clothes, designer clothes where you could get top dollar.
- Stealing cartons of cigarettes.

You name it I did it to support my habit. I traveled all over eastern N.C., going from Wilmington, Fayetteville, Wilson, Kinston, Ahoskie, Mt. Olive, New Bern etc... When you have that monkey on your back you will travel anywhere and do just about anything to support your habit.

Drug Overdose

I thought that I was unstoppable until early one Saturday morning I made another wrong decision that should've changed my mind. There I lay in the bathroom with the door locked for 6 hours; finally my family opened the door only to find blood all over the floor. I was lying on the floor with a needle in my arm. They rushed me to the hospital where I was kept for 5 days in intensive care not knowing if I would live or die. After this ordeal I begin to read the Bible that my mother bought for me, however this lasted only as long as I was in the hospital.

Crime Continues to Support
Drug Habit, Robbery etc.

As soon as I was released from the hospital I still hadn't learn my lesson and I made another wrong decision. I had to have that bag of dope and things really got worse for me. I was in and out of jail, week after week, bringing shame to my grandmother Emma. My name was blasted in the newspaper and she was too ashamed to sit on the front porch of her own home like she would do in the pass. Also I was a member of a local gang (S.C.A.G) and that didn't help matters either. I thought it was cool to belong in a gang, we were tough and no one stood in our way, we thought we were invincible, just like my father Swift.

However, after three of our gang members got killed it really begins to hit home to me. One of my cousins the leader went to prison and was given a life sentence for killing a pregnant woman and her baby. I witness these killings and it is something I will never forget, especially when one dies over someone else's tape recorder. Also when you see someone die over a chicken sandwich and another is killed by his own girlfriend. Life becomes very precious when it comes home to you. There was a young lady Angel that died of an overdose of heroin and when I think about that I have to think about the goodness of Jesus and all that he'd done for me, then my soul cries out Hallelujah! I thank God for saving me.

1977 Salvation — Received Christ into my life

I remember when my life begin to change, I was sitting under a tree as high as I could be. This young lady was on her way to church, I will never forget it, and her name was Nancy Holloway. I didn't know at the time that she was my cousin and the church she attended was The Tabernacle of Prayer for All People. The Pastor there is a great man of God name Apostle Lawrence Bogier, a man of prayer and a man of valor.

The very next day she saw me again and told me that she prayed for me. The taste of drugs was gone and I went to church and gave my heart to Jesus

Christ and I became a new creature in God. The scripture says, *"Therefore if any man be in Christ, he is a new creature: old things are passed away; behold, all things are become new."* 2 Corinthians 5:17. God begin to bless my life, at one time I could not keep a job but now I could and I begin to work and I loved to work.

Marriage and Family

In 1977 I was joined in Holy Matrimony with one of God's most wonderful creations. We were as one and it was a beautiful relationship between two people. In 1978 a third addition were added to the family and in 1979 there was a fourth addition, it was blessed and beautiful. We traveled as a family to the church events that we had like the convocation with our late Apostle Johnnie Lee Washington. We would travel to New York, Atlanta and New Orleans etc... There were great revivals during those days; our late Apostle was a man of God that was anointed. We have seen many people get saved, healed and delivered. The reverence and fear of God was upon this man and people would shake in their boots because they were thinking that the man of God would call them out. People knew that if they were living in sin he would let you know. There was no sugar coating like preachers do today, you could feel the anointing as you walk down the streets of Slocumb and Olivia lane.

During those times we saw great revival and people were getting saved and that's what a great revival does. Revival brings people to salvation; I don't know what people are calling revival these days. No one is getting saved, healed, delivered or set free. However, if I never see another great revival I haves seen one in my day. A true revival brings change to a city and in our day God used one man that made a difference. He was a true Apostle not a man made Apostle like we see in this day. Today, we have Apostles that has one church under them and some don't even have a church. True Apostles establish churches from state to state and city to city. Apostle Johnnie Washington had churches all across the country and it was in the Tabernacle of Prayer where I learned the meaning of prayer. We enjoyed prayer and looked forward to the times of prayer at church.

- *"Seek the LORD and his strength, seek his face continually." 1 Chronicles 16:11*
- *"Ask, and it shall be given you; seek, and ye shall find; knock, and it shall be opened unto you." Matthew 7:7*
- *"And he spake a parable unto them to this end, that men ought always to pray, and not to faint." Luke 18:1*
- *"And the people murmured against Moses, saying, What shall we drink? And he cried unto the LORD; and the LORD shewed him a tree, which when he had*

cast into the waters, the waters were made sweet: there he made for them a statute and an ordinance, and there he proved them." *Exodus 15:24-25*

- *"**For this child I prayed**; and the LORD hath given me my petition which I asked of him." 1 Samuel 1:27*

The early church was a church of prayer but the church today has loss their prayer life. The preachers don't speak on prayer because they're not praying themselves. The late E.M. Bounds stated, *"If a preacher isn't praying at least 2 hours a day he isn't worth a dime."* This is a heavy statement to make in the midst of a society that has forgotten God.

In the book of Acts it says, *"And when they had prayed, the place was shaken where they were assembled together; and they were all filled with the Holy Ghost, and they spake the word of God with boldness." Acts 4:31* When was the last time you assembled at the house of God to worship with the saints? You may say that you don't have to go to the house of God, I can pray at home. Yes you can pray at home but the house of God is where you go to get the word of God and get strengthen by the word and by one another. You see we need each other (I will tell you more about our need for each other later). God promised to answer his children prayer, let's look at some scriptures that confirm this.

- *He shall call upon me, and I will answer him: I will be with him in trouble; I will deliver him, and honour him. " Psalms 91:15*
- *"Then shalt thou call, and the LORD shall answer; thou shalt cry, and he shall say, Here I am. If thou take away from the midst of thee the yoke, the putting forth of the finger, and speaking vanity." Isaiah 58:9*
- *And it shall come to pass, that before they call, I will answer; and while they are yet speaking, I will hear. " Isaiah 65:24*
- *"If my people, which are called by my name, shall humble themselves, and pray, and seek my face, and turn from their wicked ways; then will I hear from heaven, and will forgive their sin, and will heal their land." 2 Chronicles 7:14*
- *"And ye shall seek me, and find me, when ye shall search for me with all your heart." Jeremiah 29:13*
- *"Therefore I say unto you, What things soever ye desire, when ye pray, believe that ye receive them, and ye shall have them. " Mark 11:24*
- *"Confess your faults one to another, and pray one for another, that ye may be healed. The effectual fervent prayer of a righteous man availeth much." James 5:16*
- *"And whatsoever we ask, we receive of him, because we keep his commandments, and do those things that are pleasing in his sight." 1 John 3:22*

Prayer comes on conditions of successful contrition's. Learn to pray your whole heart in prayer and pray in righteousness. Also, through prayer I learned how to have private devotions in Christ.

Morning Devotions

I was getting off work at 2:15 a.m. in the morning and would go to church every night. Some brothers and I were working at Kemp Furniture at the time and it was good because it gave us opportunity to spend some early devotions with God. In the scripture it says, *"And in the morning, rising up a great while before day, he went out, and departed into a solitary place, and there prayed." Mark 1:35*

Evening Prayer

Evening prayer was at 7:00 p.m. at the church before the service started. Each service was preceded by 1 hour of prayer. During that time the brothers were at the altar crying out to God, just to name a few that helped me on my journey there was:

- Elder Haywood Williams
- Elder Tommy Artis
- Elder Kornegay
- Elder Roger Taylor
- Elder Jones
- Elder Donald Wells
- Elder Sutton

- Elder Thornton
- Elder Eddie Bogier
- Pastor Joseph Watson
- Paul Horton
- Leroy Kornegay

These were brothers that Apostle Bogier could depend on, these brothers did not just carry a title they were faithful and consistent. A title meant something and these brothers were first partakers and that's where I am today, they made you accountable for your actions. The scripture tells us about evening prayer saying, *"And when he had sent them away, he departed into a mountain to pray."* Mark 6:46

We also had all night prayer and shut-ins from Friday night until early Sunday morning. We prayed through and it was not a time of sleep, the leaders don't have these kinds of all night prayers and shut-ins anymore. Many leaders don't have people around them that are prayer warriors anymore; many leaders are more concerned with tithes than tarrying. Today when a prayer meeting is called in many churches the leaders themselves are not there.

When I was coming up in the Tabernacle of Prayer they set a great example in prayer, the brothers was on post and so was the leader. Many times the brothers had already talked about the message before the Apostle came forth with the message. That's how close of a walk with God they had in prayer. Thank you Jesus, that's the gospel truth, if you don't believe it ask some of the Elders that I mentioned above, this is no fairy tale, prayer was key.

The scripture talks about all night prayer on several occasions saying, *"And it came to pass in those days, that he went out into a mountain to pray, and continued all night in prayer to God." Luke 6:12 "And being in an agony he prayed more earnestly: and his sweat was as it were great drops of blood falling down to the ground." Luke 22:44 "Peter therefore was kept in prison: but prayer was made without ceasing of the church unto God for him." Acts 12:5*

1988 – Life of Struggling and Backsliding

For twelve strong years life was good for me and I ran hard for the Lord. It was blessed and beautiful while it lasted, then a crisis came that threw me for a loop. What happened? I took my eyes off of Jesus and put them back on the world. I stopped seeking God like I once did and I failed to put the cross to the things of the world. Before you do anything make sure to apply the cross before you make any decisions. Ask yourself **"what would Jesus do?"** If I touch this or that will it make me unclean? The word of God says:

- *"And what agreement hath the temple of God with*

idols? for ye are the temple of the living God; as God hath said, I will dwell in them, and walk in them; and I will be their God, and they shall be my people. Wherefore come out from among them, and be ye separate, saith the Lord, and touch not the unclean thing; and I will receive you. And will be a Father unto you, and ye shall be my sons and daughters, saith the Lord Almighty." 2 Corinthians 6:16-18

- *"Be ye not unequally yoked together with unbelievers: for what fellowship hath righteousness with unrighteousness? and what communion hath light with darkness?" 2 Corinthians 6:14*

I laid down in the lap of Delilah and woke up with the strength of God sapped right out of me, because I love my selfish ways. I was still carnal minded, plain and simple and finally sin had conceived its mission and my decision was made and put into action. It was another wrong decision but when you're in sin you really don't care. One day my wife gets home from work and a truck from the pawn shop is at the door taking away the furniture. She doesn't know what is going on and I am a husband being rebellious and going to live in adultery. She believed that I was being faithful but this sinful act caused me to have a child with a woman that was not my wife.

Will I ever see my wife again? Sure, when my girlfriend and I would argue then I would go running back to my wife, feeding off of her weakness. One day I went home and my daughter asked if I was home to stay? I broke down and cried but two weeks later I was gone again. Who can stop you in the heat of your passion? When my child was born I needed shots of cocaine just to celebrate her birth. I hadn't had that craving for 12 years, now I was back to using it every week. This led me to losing my job, wrecking my wife's car and losing one of my fingers. I stayed in the hospital for about 6 months and the insurance paid me about $10,000. I gave my mother $1,000, my girl friend $500 and in about two weeks I was broke. All my money was gone and there was nothing to show for it except a foolish drug habit. I had turned from God and my craving increased and the more it increased the bolder I became. Once again I begin to steal and rob and this became second nature again. The word of the Lord says:

- *"Then goeth he, and taketh with himself seven other spirits more wicked than himself, and they enter in and dwell there: and the last state of that man is worse than the first. Even so shall it be also unto this wicked generation." Matthew 12:45*

- *"Turn, O backsliding children, saith the LORD; for I am married unto you:" Jeremiah 3:14*

The term backsliding simply means to turn one's

back on God. Ironically, many times God's people backslide mostly after times of great blessings and prosperity. Often when God poured out incredible mercies on Israel the people soon turned away from him. In the book of Jeremiah we see an example of this:

- *"How shall I pardon thee for this? thy children have forsaken me, and sworn by them that are no gods: when I had fed them to the full, they then committed adultery, and assembled themselves by troops in the harlots' houses. They were as fed horses in the morning: every one neighed after his neighbour's wife. Shall I not visit for these things? saith the LORD: and shall not my soul be avenged on such a nation as this? Go ye up upon her walls, and destroy; but make not a full end: take away her battlements; for they are not the LORD's. For the house of Israel and house of Judah have dealt very treacherously against me, saith the LORD." Jeremiah 5:7-11*

What the Lord is saying here is that I have blessed them and favored them and now they turned their backs on me! Jeremiah describes exactly who a backslider is. His description of a backslider is someone who once enjoyed the blessings and favor of God. This person walked before the Lord with a devoted, humble and kind heart. They loved praying and digging into God's word, they vowed, I will serve the Lord always with all my heart and for a while they did seek the Lord faithfully. They forsook their wicked ways and delighted in the fellowship they found with other saints in the house of God. But then something began to draw their heart away from the Lord. They no longer had genuine love and rebellion crept in instead.

A backslider is a dangerous person to be around. When you're a backslider you are one of the most dangerous persons on earth, you're a walking time bomb. When God has a controversy with a backslider it affects everyone around them. When the storm finally hits the backslider everyone is affected. The whole family suffers, the children, co-workers, friends and even strangers that are in their midst. The storm aimed at Jonah put everyone on the ship in danger.

- *"Now the word of the LORD came unto Jonah the son of Amittai, saying, Arise, go to Nineveh, that great city, and cry against it; for their wickedness is come up before me." Jonah 1:1-2*

However, instead of Jonah going to Nineveh he rebelled and ran. He fled to Joppa but you can't run from God and you can't hide. God arranged for a storm that came in upon the backslider Jonah on his cruise ship. Suddenly, without warning the crew was completely at the mercy of the storm. God had stirred up a whole sea to get one man who was in disobedience (Clifton). When I was an addict I use to say that my addiction is my sin and my problem only. I'm not hurting anyone but myself but that is a lie from the devil and the scripture prove that it is not just your problem. It is the problem of everyone that lives with you, walks with you and knows you. God is pursuing you and that makes you a dangerous person. When that man you owe money for drugs comes at you he doesn't care who is in the house or around you, he's coming blasting. Nobody lives and dies only to himself. When David sinned in numbering the Israelites he became a dangerous man. The judgment that God sent to him fell on Israel as well and a deadly storm came and 7,000 men lost their lives. David had to cry out to God, *"And David spake unto the LORD when he saw the angel that smote the people, and said, Lo, I have sinned, and I have done wickedly: but these sheep, what have they done? let thine hand, I pray thee, be against me, and against my father's house."* 2 Samuel 24:17

Likewise, many backslidden Christians are sending their co-workers to hell. At one time that person was a living testimony on the job, they kept a Bible with them everywhere they went and were eager to talk about Jesus. Our co-workers knew there was a genuine difference about us. But now those ungodly co-workers realized there has been a change and they know that their Christian colleague is backslidden. They can't explain what has happened in spiritual terms but they know something is different about the individual. Their once zealous Christian co-worker has become like them and they were their last hope. They may have mocked their co-worker at one time but secretly they thought, at least here is one person I can go to in trouble. The backslidden Christian has robbed them of their hope and taken away the little spark of faith they might have had. Now these heathen are convinced it's impossible to serve God and the backslider has become filled with their own ways and has become a danger to their very souls.

- *"So the shipmaster came to him (Jonah), and said unto him, What meanest thou, O sleeper? arise, call upon thy God, if so be that God will think upon us, that we perish not." Jonah 1:6*

I can imagine what the prophet Jonah thought when he awoke. He felt the rocking of the ship, heard the men wailing in fear, saw the ship filling with water. He had to be thinking uh-oh, this is it, God has caught up with me and I'm the cause of this awful storm. So he hurried up on deck to confess, he said, *"men, this is about me, I'm a backslider running from God, for I know for my sake this great tempest is upon you. Then were the men exceedingly afraid, and said unto him. Why hast thou done this? For the men knew that he fled from the presence of the LORD, because he had told them."*

Jonah 1:12, 10

The Apostle Paul also suffered through a storm at sea but it wasn't because he was running from God, Paul was at peace with God and he could stand confidently as his ship began to break apart. He could reassure the ungodly crew and tell them don't worry gentlemen – not one of you will be lost. I heard from my God last night and he has told me we're all going to be saved. If you're a backslider you probably remember a time when you could stand confidently in any storm or crisis just like Paul, you could tell the world "My God is able."

God is going to take you down into the lowest pit if you running from him like Jonah and I did. You will be swallowed up in a great trial, trust me. Your trial could be your health, your finances or your family. Yet it will happen not because God wants to destroy you or your surroundings but because you are his and you are destined for him. Accept it right now, no man or woman who runs from God escapes the storm and no human power can deliver from it. *"Then said they unto him, What shall we do unto thee, that the sea may be calm unto us? for the sea wrought, and was tempestuous. And he said unto them, Take me up, and cast me forth into the sea; so shall the sea be calm unto you: for I know that for my sake this great tempest is upon you. Nevertheless the men rowed hard to bring it to the land; but they could not: for the sea wrought, and was tempestuous against them." Jonah 1:11-13*

These ungodly sailors tried to spare Jonah, likewise my friend tried to spare me from drugs, crime, etc... But beloved when God goes after a backslider no one can hinder his divine plan. If you're running from the Lord you can mark it down your crisis is coming and it will be the storm of your life. God has already made up his mind and he has a purpose in sending the storm.

You can give in to the hopelessness and convince yourself that God hates you for your disobedience and believe in your mind that you are so far down that you can never get back to God. You can say there is no hope for me, but I want to let you know that God has ordained a mission for you and I and he would never have let me die down there. No, God could have found someone else for Jonah and Clifton mission; we all have a free will to choose. When everything is against you and when you descend to the lowest pit, feeling swallowed up by despair, you think God has abandoned you and you'll be tempted to say it's no use. God doesn't care and he can't possibly love me because he allowed all this trouble to fall on me.

But beloved, I want you to know that you can call on God for mercy, you can come back to the Lord no matter how far you've run. *"Then Jonah (Clifton) prayed unto the LORD his God out of the fish's belly, And said, I cried by reason of mine affliction unto the LORD, and he heard me; out of the belly of hell cried I, and thou heardest my voice." "This poor man cried, and the LORD heard him, and saved him out of all his troubles." "The LORD redeemed the soul of his servants, and none of them that trust in him shall be desolate." Jonah 2:1-2, Psalms 34:6, Psalms 34:22*

2

Life Change — August 2, 1992

James Street was once a very popular street in Goldsboro. The watchful eye of God was observing my every movement and pointed me to James Street. In Goldsboro it was called the block and you could get anything you wanted on the block, however this place is now closed down. The dates and year will forever be in my memory I was high on heroin and looking for cocaine. I had no idea that at the end of this dusty dark path the end closer than I thought. While on James Street I was looking for one sign but God had another sign set up for me. A preacher name Tim and a Pastor name Kirby was sent by God to speak words to me that my sin soaked soul was longing to hear.

The Lord is so good to me. He loves you but he hates sin and he is married to the backslider. God knows where you are and he wants to bring you back into the fold. Why don't you come back home to God, you see God has a special house just for you. He doesn't care what you've been through or what you may have done, his arms is stretched out still. At one time I was sleeping in the park at night, Mina Weil in the dugout, nobody knew but God. They invited me to come to church on Sunday morning. I knew that these men were really sincere, honest and full of compassion and really cared about me. So I said ok I'll be there Sunday morning. Early that Sunday morning I awoke and called the Church for a ride but I got no answer. I begin to reason how I should stay home so I laid back down and I begin to toss and turn; I couldn't get comfortable and the fan that I was using to cool off my dear mother took it to her room. So here I am miserable as can be thinking what can I do? I got up took me a nice clean shower and walked to church about 3 miles away. The scripture says, *"One thing have I desired of the LORD, that will I seek after; that I may dwell in the house of the LORD all the days of my life, to behold the beauty of the LORD, and to enquire in his temple." Psalms 27:4*

JACOB'S HOUSE

At the end of the service the Pastor spoke to me about the Jacobs house and asked if I would give it a chance with God's help. Normally they required a two week waiting period and you would come to the church service if possible for two weeks. Then they would consider you as a possible candidate. But for me (thank God) they took me in right away. I would have probably left that church that same day and went out and robbed somebody or did whatever I had to do to get another high. But God knew that and praise the Lord and they took me in. I was changed by God, I got sick and went through a time of withdrawal and it was hard. But God saw me through as he placed the brothers of the house by my side. They strengthen me with prayers and counseled me and in 6 days I was completely delivered. I was set free by the power of God, the drug life was behind me and the streets life was gone. In Matthew 7:7 it says, *"Ask, and it shall be given you. Seek, and ye shall find; knock and it shall be opened to you."* However, there still remained something that had to be faced even though my life was changed and I lived in the Jacob's House.

Reaping Time

While I was in the house there still remained the greatest challenge of all. I would meet face to face with a person that I never wanted to confront and that person was me. I believe that is the hardest thing to admit but in a program such as this where discipline is enforced it is a tremendous help. People are constantly around, you sleep with them in the same rooms, eat with them and sooner or later your true self will show and you must deal with it. If you will be honest with yourself and don't hide then God will give you the victory over that thing in your life (self). For so many years self held sway over me and I was alone and helpless to conquer, there were 4 obstacles that God helped me to overcome.

While in the Jacob's House I had to go through a completion course. It consisted of 13 courses and I finished them all and through my accomplishments was able to teach as an intern in the house. This course is part of the Group Studies National by Teen Challenge Curriculum. This course certificate is to give recognition to those who complete all the required work. I received 13 certificates of achievement. Those certificates were:

1. Growing through failure.
2. Obedience to man.
3. Obedience to God.
4. Spiritual power and supernatural.
5. Attitudes.
6. Group studies for new Christians.
7. A quick look at the Bible.
8. How can I know I'm a Christian?
9. Personal rights.
10. Successful Christian living
11. How to study the Bible.
12. Temptation.
13. Personal relationships with others.

All of these courses help to make me what I am today and they help to lay a foundation in me through the word of God.

During the program I couldn't work on a regular job making my own money. You had to be in the program for at least 6 months before you can even think about a job and then you could only work part time. When I was shooting drug and sleeping in the park I didn't even think about working a job and then all of a sudden I wanted to work. This was just a trick of the enemy to try and take my rest before I even got started well. But the race is not given to the swift but he that endures to the end and I was going to endure this thing which was me.

I begin to think that the program was treating me like a child. You have someone always having to tell you what to do, transport you where you have to go and always questioning your motives. But when you're out there in the world doing your thing, riding with other people, going into stores stealing even then someone is telling you what to do and asking you questions. Even in the world people were questioning your motives asking you did you do the best when you went in the store. Are you holding out any money from the money bag you ripped off at the store when the clerk went in the back? Someone is always questioning you and there was no trust and I begin to feel just like this in the Jacob's young intern program because it was like they were watching your every move.

During the intern there were men that were younger than I was and I was like a father in age to some of them. I looked at these guys and asked what do they know? I didn't want to submit to this authority. One of the rules was that you had to be in bed at a certain time. The lights were off and you had to share with either one or two others. You couldn't leave anything out not even anything under the beds, not even your shoes. There was no TV, no newspapers, no radio and I thought this is too much, but God saw me through and he broke the chains and gave me the grace to stay in, *"for with God nothing shall be impossible." Luke 1:37*

Favor of God — Court System

There were still some things that I had to confront that happened before I came to the Jacob's house. I faced another charge that I didn't know about or I just forgot that I did it. I never thought that the person would press charges against me, but I did a terrible thing. I faced arm robbery with a sawed off shotgun. I had been in the Jacob's house for 3 months and some of the brothers and I was helping a sister from the church to move. As we were on Ash Street leaving Hardees's the policemen stopped us and asked for some identification. I didn't have any kind of I.D. on me so he asked the driver for his I.D... The policemen told us that we fit the description of three guys who has just robbed someone in front of the Wachovia Bank. He eventually let us go but first he ran a check on the truck belonging to one of the guys that was in the Air Force. He gave the officers our names and they soon discovered that there was a warrant for my arrest and the charge was armed robbery.

At first I couldn't believe it and they took me down and booked me for armed robbery with a sawed off shotgun. I was put under a $75,000 bond and I knew the church was not going to stand that bond, besides I was only there for 3 months. They didn't know me like that but God knows everything about me. Therefore I decided to just see what my outcome would be. That was the first time in my life that I had ever gone to jail and prison and I have been too many jails in N.C. in my life. I went to a jail in Kinston and it was dark you couldn't see anything and I said if hell is worse than this Lord help us.

I had a rap sheet 2 pages long but I was confident because God was in my life and I knew that everything would be fine. I had joy, unspeakable joy and full of the Holy Ghost. I called the Jacob's House that night and asked that the staff could bring me a book by the great Corrie Ten Boom, Marching for the End Time Battle. That following morning I had to go before the Judge for my first appearance. I looked beyond my cell bars to see my Pastor (Danny Kirby) and a lawyer. The District Attorney and the Judge began to discuss the case and the amount of money that the church could give. At that point God allowed the Director to talk about the program and he talked for 5 minutes, it doesn't take God all day to get the job done. The Judge wanted to know what could the church afford for my bond and they stated about $75. The D.A. was against it and he protested and stated that I deserve a higher bond.

Because of the nature of the crime and my past record he stated that my rap sheet showed that I was a great risk. Nevertheless, the Judge was quite impressed with the program and he was astonished with the dramatic decrease of the bond. I remember the Judge saying, "I want to see you make it." I had to report to court seven months later and went I showed up my lawyer told me that they were offering me a plea bargain for a lesser charge. The offer was 10 years in prison so I told my lawyer to give me some time to think about it and I would get back with him later.

I went to talk with my Pastor in order to get godly counsel and he told me that in order to get favor with God I had to go to court and admit that I was guilty of the crime. So I told my lawyer that I wanted to plead guilty and take my chances. My lawyer was hesitant and he told me that with my record I was looking at forty years but he may be able to get me 10 years. I told him to do whatever he thought was best. So my lawyer went in and began to bargain with the Judge, once again the D.A. began to talk about how I needed to serve some time in prison. He begin to say that the nature of my crime was with a sawed off shot gun and that I meant to hurt the plaintiff. But my lawyer talked with the Judge about how this program that I was in was helping me tremendously. My lawyer even brought in the Director (Tim) of the program to share his thoughts about the program with the Judge. The Judge became quite interested in the program and I knew that it was only the hand of God that touched the heart of the Judge. The Judge asked the D.A. what did the state recommend and of course the D.A. said I needed prison time. He asked the plaintiff what did he think and he said "the program is working for Mr. Battle." I forgive him for robbing me with the shot gun and I don't think he deserve any time Judge. The Judge said stand up Mr. Battle, I can't just let you off the hook without giving you some kind of punishment. I sentence you to weekend jail for three months and afterwards six months of house arrest (God is Good). House arrest was really no problem at all, I could still do the things that I enjoyed such as going to church and visiting my children during the weekdays. I had to be in by 10:30 p.m. On weekends I had to be in by 1:30 a.m. (that's right 1:30 a.m.). Nobody can do you like Jesus, nobody. When I share this testimony with others they find it very hard to believe but my Bible tells me, *"For with God nothing shall be impossible."* *Luke 1:37*

Graduation from the Jacob's House

I graduated from the Jacob's House in about 13

months and it was a great day in my life. I thought I couldn't make it but God gave me grace to run the race. The race is not given to the swift, but to him that endure to the end. God also had me at the Jacob's House to be a witness to other brothers that would be coming into the house. These brothers would have pretty much the same problems that I was delivered from. Many friends of mine that I knew on the streets came to the house and when they saw how God had blessed and delivered me it gave them hope. Many men come in with no hope at all but God had me in the right place at the right time.

I finally got my degree and several awards and what really blessed me was that my family was there to see me graduate. All were there and it blessed me so much:

- My mother
- Children
- Brothers
- Sisters
- Nieces
- Nephews
- Grandchildren

I didn't have that many people to come see me on my graduation from High School, I broke down and cried and it felt so good. These tears were tears of joy and the joy that God gives you the world can't take it away. My grandmother Lucy Swift was 83 years old at the time and she was so proud of me, she wrote me a letter telling me to stick it out and that God loves me. That letter made a great impact on my life and it still blesses me today, it really touched my soul down on the inside, hallelujah, praise God.

JACOB'S HOUSE

Lord I give you praise because you are worthy to be praised, your name is above every name, Lord I bless your name. I can't help but give him praise, look where he has brought me from, he didn't have to do it but he did. I was minding my own business and God chose me and handpicked me out of the crowd. He chose me out of all my friends, Lord why choose me? I may not understand now but I will fulfill my destiny. Thank you Lord for bringing me out of darkness into your marvelous light, I got to praise you. Lord I was like Paul, blind on my way to hell but you placed my foot on the solid rock and that rock is Jesus Christ. After my graduation I decided to stay on as an intern.

Intern

As an intern you have certain privileges that you don't have being a student. I loved being an intern and as an intern I had the privilege of learning how the brothers feel on certain issues in the house. I let the brothers know that it's not so much about the house but it's about them. Once you deal with that old man standing in the mirror in the morning you can make it. That old man has to die to the flesh, the word of God says, *"For we know that the law is spiritual: but I am carnal, sold under sin. For that which I do I allow not: for what I would, that do I not; but what I hate, that do I. If then I do that which I would not, I consent unto the law that it is good. Now then it is no more I that do it, but sin that dwelleth in me. For I know that in me (that is, in my flesh,) dwelleth no good thing: for to will is present with me; but how to perform that which is good I find not. For the good that I would I do not: but the evil which I would not, that I do. Now if I do that I would not, it is no more I that do it, but sin that dwelleth in me. I find then a law, that, when I would do good, evil is present with me." Romans 7:14-21*

It's not easy but with God's help you can do it, forget about the rules and remember why you're there and why you came. You came to get some discipline in your life. A drug addict is just like a baby, when you turn your back they will get into trouble. You have to watch them 24/7. I enjoyed being an intern because I loved helping the brothers, encouraging them to hold out.

God also blessed me with a job making good money; I was making over $11.00 an hour back in the early 90's. I bought a car and God was blessing me beyond measure. I had my own room in the house and my own phone. I didn't have to be in bed at a certain time and could cut out the lights when I wanted to. I stayed on to be an intern for about 9 months or so, when you reach a certain level you got to pray for wisdom and understanding so that you can stay in God's divine will. I kept praying to God and he let me know that it was time to move on; this was the hardest decision I ever had to make so far. But I got my answer from God that my destiny had come to an end at the Jacob's House and it was time for me to leave.

Life Today

In the book of Isaiah 45:2 it says, *"I will go before thee, and make the crooked places straight: I will break in pieces the gates of brass, and cut in sunder the bars of iron."* In Isaiah 35:8 it says, *"And an highway shall be there, and a way, and it shall be called The way of holiness."*Lord show me the right way. *"Thou wilt shew me the path of life: in thy presence is fulness of joy; at thy right hand there are pleasures for evermore."* Psalms 16:11 One Sunday morning being led by the Holy Spirit I was inspired to visit one of my best friends on planet earth in a small country town called Windsor (Pastor Joseph Watson and Family). He had a church and God was blessing it and moving by his Spirit. This was not a fleshy church but a spiritual church like the one I was raised up in (Hallelujah). I was blessed on that Sunday when I visited and afterwards I would go back home to Goldsboro when the service was over. This was a 2 hour drive one way but it didn't matter about the distance because I was enjoying Jesus.

I was working at this job in Goldsboro called A.P. Parts and I was working on the third shift from Sunday night till Thursday night. A friend and I (sister Bessie) would travel every Sunday to go to the service. I was praying to God for direction about what he wanted me to do, however, I didn't know that the Pastor was also praying that God would send someone to start a:

- Prison ministry

- Rest home ministry

- Street ministry and

- Mission for Christ

One Sunday I missed a service and the Pastor told the congregation that God had sent that young man (Clifton) to do a work that he has been praying for. Pastor never told me what God had said to him, a lady from the church told me how Pastor had stood up and said what God was going to do. Pastor is a man of prayer. When God tell you something you don't have to say a word, God will send a confirmation.

As time went on my job had a big layoff and I begin to draw unemployment which amounted to about $300 a week. I wasn't ready to go back to work so the Lord opened up the door to my Pastor's house and I stayed with him while I was drawing unemployment. Pastor and I went to church 6 days a week. We went to early Morning Prayer at 6 a.m. and God was blessing in a great way. We had about 3 men in the church and Pastor said to me, *"Let's keep praying that God will send men in the ministry."* I know prayer works and God begin to send more men in the church. I stayed with my beloved friend for about 1 year as he opened his home to me. The scripture says, *"A man that hath friends must shew himself friendly: and there is a friend that sticketh closer than a brother." Proverbs 18:24* This is what I saw in my friend, a man of God that came to my aid when I was down and out at my lowest point in the early 90's. The Watson family showed me love; they prayed for me and came to visit me when I was in jail. However, by the time they got to the jail house I was already released. A real friend will go the last mile to help that person fulfil their destiny.

I had to do some ground work to start the mission for Christ. We would visit:

- Odom Farm

- Eastern

- Gates Co.

- Martin Co.

- Bertie Correctional

- Fountain Correctional

They had closed down some of the prisons, but Minister Battle and Wife had started about 6 Rest

Home Ministries at this time. We had 4 in Windsor, 2 in Ahoskie, we still visit Rest homes but not as much as we use to. I told God I need someone to help me in this ministry, I need a help mate, someone that would pray for me and pray for the ministry, a lady that would have the same spirit and love for people as I do. And God said Clifton you don't have to look any further, she is right there with you and she has been there the whole time. I could not believe it, God bless me with a wonderful beautiful creature, one that prays not just talks about prayer. God bless me to marry Mrs. Brenda Barnes on August 12th 1995. This wonderful lady helped me get my first drivers license back in 1975. We had been friends for a long time before I married my sweetheart. I never touched her until I said I do (wow).

When my unemployment ran out God had a job and a house waiting for me before I got married. As I begin to fulfil my destiny things begin to happen, prayer was a serious part of my life and some mornings in 1998 I would spend 3 hours in prayer before I went to work. Many times I didn't understand what God was doing in prayer but he was preparing me. I had a custom or calling for Morning Prayer, at work the young ladies would come and we would join hands in prayer before we started on the line to work. If I forgot they would say, Bro. Clifton we still having prayer aren't we, they had a thirst for prayer.

While at work one day I had been working for about 2 hours when the boss called me off the lines and said Clifton come and go with me. So I followed him to the wellness center and when I got there my wife and my Pastor were there. They said Clifton I have to tell you something, your daughter Comeshia have been in a wreck and they totalled the vehicle and your daughter died. She was the only one that died, there were four other people in the car.

God is a burden bearer and heavy load carrier; he let me lean on him. God knew that I was going to need someone to lean on; he let me hold back the tears he had prepared me for that. The foreman said Clifton it's alright to cry but I told him that I was alright. So we had to go and I.D. the body in Raleigh, N.C. That was hard on me, when I saw her body in the morgue I broke down and cried like a baby, I couldn't control myself. But I had comfort in the scriptures and according to Romans 8:28 it says, *"And we know that all things work together for good to them that love God, to them who are the called according to his purpose."*

Around November 28th 1999 I had another tragedy to enter my life, I lost my dear sister Angela, she was so dear to me and when she died I broke down in tears. My sister and I became very close and when she got sick I would go to the hospital and read and pray for her. She really enjoyed those times as I read the scriptures and prayed for her, when she got sick it was like I got sick. That was my sister fatty, I loved her and she loved me, we were knitted together. I really miss my sister and the devil was really trying me, telling me to give up. First I lost my daughter then my sister and also my dearest grandmother in 1995. Lucy Swift always prayed for me and I did have a chance to visit her in Philadelphia, before she died. She was in the Rest Home and she encouraged me once again to hold on to God and a few months later God called her home, thank God for grandmother prayers.

Sometimes pain comes and you don't understand the struggles you're going through and why. Once again death hit my family, my cousin that was raised with me was like a sister to me and I was raised up in the same house with her. In 2001 she died and I begin to cry out to God, Lord what are you trying to show me. Trouble hit home once again when my precious mother was called home to be with the Lord in 2003. Before she was called home she had already lost both of her legs and she was in so much pain. Well thank God where she is now she has no more pain and suffering. I remember how she was telling the family about how I was out of control and it was bothering her. She had done all she could do and she told God to either kill me or save me. Mother knew the power of God and on one occasion when Apostle Johnnie Washington was running a tent revival on Slocumb St in Goldsboro, NC, she got some sawdust from under the tent and put it in her purse. When she got home that night she put it all on me but I was so high I didn't feel a thing. But I can tell you that Holy Ghost sawdust works when the ground you walk on is holy. I miss my mom prayers but I am glad that she got the chance to see me come back to God.

Thank God I was able to get my fight back, if you settle things with God everything else will fall in line. You see when you're right before God and sprinkled with Christ's blood and no sin in your life and prevailing in prayer all the demons in hell can't make a dent in what God wants to do in your life. That same year while working on a step ladder somehow my feet came from under me and I fell. I had to have surgery on my back; there were 2 level decompressions on the left at L4-5 and L5-51. The surgical procedure was performed at Pitt County Memorial Hospital in 2005. That same year I lost a brother and right before he died I lost a sweet sister in law (Carlene), she got in her car and just died at the steering wheel, she had a heart attack.

In 2007 I had my first heart attack, I was on my way

to Goldsboro and I had gotten as far as Snow Hill, it was around 4:30 a.m. I pulled over to the store to buy me a newspaper and started feeling really bad. I got back into the car and started feeling really funny; I had pain in my chest that I never felt before. I told some man that had stopped to call the Ambulance and that is all that I can remember. I woke up with a stein in me.

In 2008 I was on my way to Chicago to visit my son Stanley and while at the airport I was feeling pretty bad. When I got to his house I lay down but the pain would not go away so they called the Ambulance. When I got to the hospital I found out that I need bypass surgery. When I got back home I went back to Pitt Memorial Hospital to get it done.

In 2009 tragedy struck once again when I lost another brother (Dennis). However, the consolation that I have is that I will see my two brothers, grandmother, mother, daughter and sister again because they were saved. I know that if I live right and hold on I will see them again in heaven. Lord help me to hold out till my change come.

Truly I have seen my share of car accidents and God's faithfulness:

- I lost control of my car on Republican Rd. in Windsor, NC. I hit a light pole and found myself in the field.

- Another time I turned my car over in a ditch.

- Another time on my way to Goldsboro I just dropped off my daughter and grandson, drove down William St. and fell asleep at the wheel. When I awoke I was going head on with another car but God allowed the car to go to the other side. I hit two light poles splitting both in half, a fire hydrant and came out without a scratch.

- On another occasion I hit a school bus and total loss my car but there were no kids on the bus, walked out with no scratches.

- Coming from Atlanta, Ga. in a snowstorm we made it all the way to Raleigh, NC, encountering 18 wheelers that had lost control. Some of them were in trees and even though we had an accident also I wasn't driving on this occasion. I guess God wanted me to see his faithfulness in all I went through. In this accident we were headed down a deep hill and I saw death for the first time. There was a tree there to stop us from going over, five people were in the car and three of us called out to God for help at the same time and help showed up.

All together I total loss three cars and have various ailments that I've had to deal with or am dealing with at this time. Ailments such as:

1. Carpal Tunnel in both hands.

2. Back Surgery

3. Three Heart Attacks

4. Bypass Surgery

5. Gout

6. Coronary Artery Disease

7. Mixed Hyperlipedemia

8. Hypercholes Terolemia

9. Sleep Apnea

10. Congestive Heart Failure

11. Diabetes

12. Hypertension

13. Arthritis

14. Shoulder Super

15. Had my blood turn to syrup

I have seen my share of sickness and diseases and on many occasions I didn't know if I would even make it. But thank God for a wonderful helpmeet that stood by my side every day. Thank God for a wife that prayed for me through these physical battles and is still by my side today. The word of God lets us know that every trial is not a test, in the book of Revelation 2:9 it tells us that God takes no delight in testing his children. The Bible says that Christ is sympathetic towards us in all our trials and he can be touched with the feelings of our infirmities. He tells the Church that I know thy tribulation and poverty. I know what you're going through, you may not understand it but I know all about it.

Everyone that follows Jesus is going to face tribulations. In Psalms 34:19 it says, *"Many are the afflictions of the righteous."* In Psalms 11:5 it says, *"The Lord trieth the righteous."* The Bible has a great deal to say about suffering, trials and troubles in the lives of believers.

- *"My soul is full of troubles." Psalms 88:3a*

- *"Enduring great and sore troubles." Psalms 71:20a*

- *"The sorrows of death compassed me, and the pains of hell got hold upon me. I found troubles and sorrow.*

- *"We looked for peace, but no good came, and for a time of health and behold troubles." Jeremiah 18:15*

Every Christian has to know and accept that God has a purpose in all our sufferings. No test comes into our life without God allowing it and one of God's purposes behind our trials is to produce an unwavering faith, *"that the trial of your faith, being much more precious than that of gold that perisheth, though it be tried with fire, might be found unto praise and honor and glory at appearing of Jesus Christ." 1 Peter 1:71*

Paul was afflicted but he knew he still had work to do. There were trials and sufferings ahead of him but he was able to say, *"I may not have apprenhended Christ as I wanted and haven't perfected. But when it comes to faith, and trusting God through every trial, I know whom I have believed and I am (Clifton) persuaded."* When the enemy came into my life like a flood I know without a doubt that God lifted up a standard against him and that's why Clifton is standing today. Can you still look to heaven and say, I know the Lord is good and I'm going to trust him through this.

A test is not always God's purpose behind our trials; the more you walk close to Christ and the deeper your trials the more he is working in you to accomplish something other than faith. Your trials are going to end and your troubles will pass away. Therefore don't focus on those things but focus your eyes on Christ and set your affections on spending eternity with him in the new world. The trials that man are enduring right now isn't testing, it's training. We're being prepared for a world where there will be no more pain therefore it's very important how we react in our present everyday trials. I therefore rejoice in my sufferings. Colossians 1:23-24

3

Fulfilling Your Destiny

Destiny is God's purpose for your life; it is your appointed and ordained future. Destiny is what God has predetermined you to be and it is his divine will that you become that. Saul was a man that missed his destiny, God himself chose Saul to lead Israel out of bondage to the Philistines. In 1 Samuel 9:17 it says, *"Behold the man whom I spake to thee of! this same shall reign over my people."* Samuel didn't choose Saul, nor did Israel choose him but God said I have appointed this man. Saul was touched by God, appointed by God, moved upon by the Holy Spirit, gifted with a spirit of prophecy and destined by God to lead Israel.

God was with him. Saul started out right and for a while he lived his destiny and walked in the fear of God. He won many great battles and was appointed King over Israel. One of Saul's most tragic pictures in all of scriptures is when he began to fall apart. He had walked in his destiny for only a short time yet God fully intended that Saul would live out the rest of his days with the Lord's blessings. He wanted Saul to be remembered as the man who delivered Israel from the bondage of the Philistines. However, Saul missed his destiny and he begin to make compromises to attain things and he missed the plan that God had for his life. Saul stated, *"God is departed from me, and answereth me no more, neither by prophets, nor by dreams: therefore I have called thee, that thou mayest make known unto me what I shall do. 1 Samuel 28:15b* By Saul's own confession he states that God is no longer with him. A man can be called by God and have the blessings and anointing of God upon him and then go off track and end up being abandon by God. Don't become a person who misses their destiny.

Samson was another man that was destined by God but also missed his destiny. In Judges 13:5 it says, *"And he shall begin to deliver Israel out of the hand of the Philistines."* This man was predestined by God and Angels announced his birth by giving his parents detailed instructions on how to raise him. Samson was to be a Nazarene, meaning he was to be given completely to God's service for his entire life. He was never to drink wine or cut his hair and he was never to touch anything dead. He couldn't even go to the funeral of a near relative. Samson was raised under strict training. At a young age he experienced the moving of God's Spirit upon him.

What is the first thing the Holy Spirit does when he moves on us? He convicts of Sin, Righteousness and Judgment. The Holy Spirit guides, comforts and teaches us, he prays through us with cries, groaning and supplications. If you would have met Samson when he was young he probably would have told you, God said I am someone special. I've also had God's Spirit to come upon me and I was called to be a Nazarene. Samson knew he had a destiny and that he was born for a purpose, he was called to bring deliverance to Israel. Samson walked in his destiny for 20 years and in obedience to God he saw the mighty works of God. You have to understand that Samson strength was not in his hair but in the moving of God's Spirit upon him. Without the Spirit of God upon him he would have been as weak as you or I. Samson missed his destiny because his heart was black with sin. He kept up an outward holiness but he chased after harlots. When he went down to see Delilah he was flirting with danger and although the Spirit moved upon Samson he never allowed the Spirit to touch his inner man.

Samson should have lived out his days as a vessel of honor and he should have experienced one victory after another for Israel and his own life. We see a man that ended up as one of the most pitiful weaklings in biblical history. In the end we see Samson strapped unto a harness like a dumb ox, his eyes gauged out and he had lost all his strength. He is the laughing stock of the heathen and his own people have turned against him. Samson ended up being a man that missed his destiny.

We can compare our destiny to that of any person in the Old or New Testament but God is doing an entirely new thing. Because of the cross of Jesus Christ God has given us a better covenant with better promises. God has gathered up all the destinies of mankind into one grand purpose. He placed them all in his Son according to Ephesians 1:10 stating, *"That in the dispensation of the fullness of times he might gather together in one all things in Christ, both which are in heaven, and which are on earth; even in him."* God has gathered all our destinies in Jesus so that his Son would have pre-eminence. Today there are no more individual destinies but one destiny for all believers, yes you do have a destiny and it is the same as mine.

It doesn't matter whether you're an Apostle, Bishop, Carpenter, Barber, Doctor or Nurse; we all have the same fixed predetermined destiny given to us before the world began. In the book of Ephesians 1:4-6 it states, *"According as he hath chosen us in him before the foundation of the world, that we should be holy and without blame before him in love: Having predestinated us unto the adoption of children by Jesus Christ to himself, according to the good pleasure of his will, To the praise of the glory of his grace, wherein he hath made us accepted in the beloved."*

God says that in the last days in the fullness of time he has one divine purpose and that is for every follower to come into adoption by Jesus Christ. God wants his people to be blameless and to the praise of his glory. *"In whom also we have obtained an inheritance, being predestinated according to the purpose of him who worketh all things after the counsel of his own will: That we should be to the praise of his glory, who first trusted in Christ."* Ephesians 1:11-12 Our destiny is to be adopted children of God, we have been adopted by the heavenly Father and the devil no longer has any claim on us. We are to live for our Lord, blameless and holy by the power of God's Spirit. Our single purpose on this earth is to live our lives as a praise and glory to him. It's not your destiny to:

- Start a prison ministry

- Rest home ministry

- Street ministry

- A house for drug addiction like Jacob House

My destiny has little to do with the things that God has allowed me to do now or later. My destiny has been to walk as an adopted son of God living before the world blameless, all to his praise and glory. When I came to Windsor nothing changed, my destiny had remained to build up the body of Christ and to walk before the Lord as an adopted son. The things that we obtain on earth will not be standing one day. The ministries that we engage in are simply burdens of the Lord that God allowed us to share and undertake. As we walk in our destiny of doing his perfect will God will bless the ministries that we partake of as long as we live in our destiny.

Beloved, if you're going to walk in your destiny the only thing that will set you apart is your desire to surpass all others in the knowledge of Jesus, no one will spend more time alone with him than you.

On Judgment day not one word will be said of mighty works, there will be no notice of personal fame or success of human accomplishments. Instead the question will be:

- Did you grow in Christ?

- Did you allow the Holy Spirit to teach you to serve others?

- Did you give up your rights?

- What were you like at home?

So are you fulfilling your destiny? Are you more like Jesus this year than you were last year? Do people see the love of Jesus in you? What will be written on your tombstone? Will it be the person who missed their destiny or the person who walked humbly with their God? Will it be said that you were a person of prayer and a person that fulfil their destiny? Destiny is not a matter of chance but a matter of choice; from this day forward choose to fulfil your destiny.

Bio: Clifton E. Battle Sr.

Minister Clifton E. Battle Sr. is a native of the Tarheel State, born and raised in Wayne County, Goldsboro, NC. He attended Dillard High School and graduated with the class of 1969. Clifton worked various jobs in Goldsboro such as:

- Kemp Furniture

- A.P. Parts

- Georgia Pacific

Clifton is married to Mrs. Rubie (Brenda) Battle and they have a total of 7 children and 9 grandchildren and 1 great grandson.

Clifton accepted Jesus Christ under the Leadership of the Late Apostle Johnnie Washington Overseer of The Tabernacle of Prayer for All People Inc., Brooklyn, NY. He continued his membership under the Leadership of Apostle Lawrence Bogier Jr. and Eldress Corethea Bogier. He attended the Tabernacle Bible Institute, taking such classes as General Bible 1 & 2, Evangelism and Christian Worker.

Later he moved to Windsor, NC where he currently attends The Church of God for All People under the Leadership of Pastor Joseph and Momma Reita Watson. He was ordained a minister under the Leadership of Pastor Watson. God has truly bless this man of God, along with his wife they have started 6 Prison Ministries and 6 Rest Home Ministries all under the Heading of Mission for Christ.

Volunteers
of The Year
2007

Presented April 17, 2008
To
Rev. Clifton & Brenda B. Battle
For Their Faithful Service
At
Odom Correctional Institution
"Volunteers Light The Way"

Minister Clifton and Brenda can be reached:

By email at: cliftonandbrenda@yahoo.com

By phone at: **252-724-0449**

www.ingramcontent.com/pod-product-compliance
Lightning Source LLC
Chambersburg PA
CBHW070916280326
41934CB00008B/1750